THE 1950s

Sally Hewitt

W

FRANKLIN WATTS
LONDON•SYDNEY

I Can Remember the 1950s

First published in 2003 by Franklin Watts
96 Leonard Street, London EC2A 4XD

Franklin Watts Australia
45-51 Huntley Street
Alexandria, NSW 2015

© Franklin Watts 2003

Series editor: Sarah Peutrill
Series design: White Design
Art director: Jonathan Hair
Picture researcher: Diana Morris

A CIP catalogue record
for this book is available from
the British Library

ISBN 0 7496 4866 X

Printed in Malaysia

Picture credits:
Advertising Archives: front cover cl; Central Press/Hulton
Archive: 6c; Corbis: 28t; Mary Evans PL: 21t, 24t; Fox/Hulton
Archive: 25b; Bert Hardy/Picture Post/Hulton Archive: 4,
16b; Hulton Archive: front cover tl, front cover cr, 7tr, 8t,
18c, 24; Kurt Hutton/Hulton Archive: 12; Keystone/Hulton
Archive: 20b; Roger Mayne/Mary Evans PL: 13b, 20t; Picture
Post/Hulton Archive: front cover b, 14-15b, 17t, 17b. Maurice Rougement/Corbis Sygma:
11c; G. Stroud/Hulton Archive: 29b; Carl Sutton/Picture Post/Hulton Archive: 23t;
Topical Press/Hulton Archive: 9b; Gerald Wilson/Mary Evans PL: 22b; Chaloner
Woods/Hulton Archive: 8b. Whilst every attempt has been made to clear copyright
should there be any inadvertent omission please apply in the first instance to the
publisher regarding rectification.

The author and publisher would
like to thank everyone who contributed
their memories and personal photographs to this book.

Contents

Introduction

THE 1950S

At the beginning of the 1950s, World War II had been over for five years, but people in Britain were still living with many of its after-effects. For the first few years of the 1950s, food was still rationed and some things such as fuel were in short supply.

NEW TOWNS

Cities suffering from bomb damage were still being rebuilt so families had the chance to move away from inner cities into modern houses in new towns such as Harlow and Stevenage.

THE WELFARE STATE

The war had brought to light the poor health and living conditions that affected many people. In 1946 the Welfare State was put into place by Clement Attlee's Labour government. It gave everyone access to free health care, education and unemployment support as well as pensions. By the 1950s, more people were enjoying better health care, education and living conditions than ever before.

NATIONAL SERVICE

Throughout the 1950s, National Service was in force. Young men aged 18 had to serve in the armed forces for two years. This was so that Britain would always have a body of trained men who could go to war at a moment's notice.

⬆ The construction of a new town in 1950. The aim was to complete 300,000 houses a year.

NEW IN THE 1950S

By the mid 1950s cars were cheaper and the roads started to get busier. Household machines began to make life easier for the housewife. Having had a taste of work during the war, more women now went out to work.

ENTERTAINMENT

People had more money than before and the cinemas were packed week after week. Television became more widespread and teenagers discovered rock 'n' roll.

THEY CAN REMEMBER

In this book six people share their memories of what it was like to live in Britain in the 1950s. They each have a story to tell in their own section, but they also add other memories throughout the book.

Then

Now

Cynthia Lacey*

At the beginning of the 1950s Cynthia was a housewife in Worthing, with three children. By the end of the decade she had five children.

* Now Cynthia Farnes

Then

Terry Cowlishaw

Terry lived in Leicester in the 1950s where he was a teenage rock 'n' roll fan.

Now

Then

Now

Teresa Martin*

Teresa was a child living in Chichester in the 1950s. She remembers what it was like at primary school. * Now Teresa James

Then

Michael Naish

Michael was a teenager living in London in the 1950s. He visited the Festival of Britain and Battersea Fun Fair.

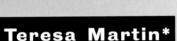

Now

Estel McDonald

Estel left Jamaica to work in the UK in 1951 to make a better life for her family.

Then

Now

Brian King

Brian, a young man in the 1950s, remembers his time doing Alternative National Service in Austria. Afterwards he moved back to the UK to resume his career as an architect.

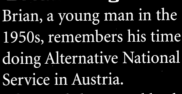

Then

Then

Now

Cynthia Lacey's story

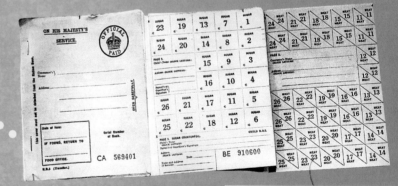

Cynthia, 1952

FOOD RATIONING

The hardship of the war years was still casting a shadow over Britain at the beginning of the 1950s. Everyone still had a ration book for basic foods such as sugar, butter, meat and tea. Cynthia was married with three little girls and remembers shopping and feeding the family.

> *Because I had grown up during the war, I was used to rations and it didn't seem much of a hardship. Rationing had been so strict you had to eat what was on your plate. If you didn't, then there was no pudding – we felt that was right.*

RATIONS END

At last, in 1954, you could throw away your ration books. Nine years after the war ended, food rationing was over.

→ Ration books contained coupons that could be exchanged for foods such as milk, sugar and sweets.

! Michael remembers...

"We had a sweet shop two doors up the road. When rationing ended I went in there having enough money to buy a lot of sweets that I never had before."

CYNTHIA BECAME A GOOD COOK

A typical meal Cynthia would cook for the family was cod with mashed potatoes, peas and broccoli followed by a steamed treacle pudding and custard.

> *There was no convenience food, it didn't exist. I could feed the family for five shillings [25 pence] very healthily.*

SHOPPING

There were no supermarkets so Cynthia pushed her two youngest girls in the pram to the local shops.

Cynthia (right) and family, 1950

> ❝ I had a twin pram, it was a Silver Cross, which would look enormous today. ❞

DELIVERIES

Local shops knew their customers well and delivered shopping by bicycle or van.

> ❝ I could phone up the butcher and say what I wanted and he would send it round. ❞

⬆ Horse-drawn carts delivered milk in churns, as shown here, and in bottles. During the 1950s, horse and carts were gradually replaced by electric milk floats.

> ❝ Milk was delivered by horse and cart. Polly the horse was a great attraction with my girls. ❞

NAPPIES

Disposable nappies were invented in America in 1956 but didn't become widely available in Britain straight away. Washing nappies was time-consuming.

> ❝ The nappies had to be boiled on the stove in a big bucket. Then you had to give them about four rinses. Then they would go out on the line to dry. It was a dreadful day when you had to dry them inside because they would go all stiff and you had to iron them to make them soft. ❞

Running the home

NEW IDEAS

Running the home gradually became easier. Household machines were more affordable. Clothes made of new materials such as nylon dried quickly and didn't need ironing. Cynthia remembers some of the new ideas.

WASHING DAY

Washing machines became more popular but they weren't very reliable. The washing could take all day, usually a Monday.

← New washing powders with detergents that could dissolve grease made washing quicker and easier.

> *I had a twin tub that used to jump all over the kitchen. I sat on it to hold it down. It was attached to the taps with hoses which would come off and shoot water everywhere.*

> *We had one of the first dishwashers. It was a very eccentric machine. In general it was more trouble than it was worth. Other people were very disapproving about us having a dishwasher.*

BEST THING SINCE SLICED BREAD

Sliced bread had been banned during the war as an economy measure. From 1950, it was back in the shops again.

↑ A 1950s kitchen with the latest equipment, including a washing machine, electric food mixer and gas cooker.

> *Sliced bread was an innovation. We thought it was slightly immoral. Some of the older generation thought it was disgusting laziness. At least the slices were straight, not all fat at one end and wobbly at the other.*

KEEPING WARM

In the 1950s, very few homes had central heating. Coal fires kept you warm and the boiler that heated the water had to be kept going all year round. Cynthia remembers lighting fires and stoking boilers.

> " In the winter, the bedrooms were icy. You just had to put on more clothes. Our boiler for heating water was solid fuel. We had stoves to heat the house all over the place, one in the hall, one in the dining room and a coal fire in the living room. "

! Estel remembers...

"At that time, you used to have fog. The terrible fog. Going to work, you'd get on the bus and the conductor had to get out to guide it – especially going round the roundabouts. You had to have a light to take you round."

Coal fires and the smog

December 1952 was very cold. Smoke from millions of coal fires poured out of chimneys all over the country as people tried to keep warm. On 5th December a sooty, smoky smog came down over London and didn't lift until 9th December.

Clean Air Act 1956

The Clean Air Act of 1956 banned the burning of coal fires in towns and cities. Only smokeless fuel could be burned. Gradually the thick, suffocating smogs disappeared altogether.

➡ Smog made driving very dangerous. This bus conductor leads the bus with a flare.

! Michael remembers...

"Smog used to creep into the house, and when it cleared you could see black sooty marks on the window sill. Our neighbour had bronchitis and every time the smogs came he was terribly ill."

Going to school

PRIMARY SCHOOL

From the outside many school buildings today look much the same as they did in the 1950s, but inside, things were very different. Teresa went to primary school in Chichester, Sussex. The infants were in a tiny classroom and the two junior classes were in a larger room, divided by a partition. There was no central heating.

> *There were two boilers in the larger classroom which were black and dirty and surrounded by rails. The caretaker would come at regular intervals during the day and restock the boilers with coal. We children had to stay well away because it was dangerous and dirty.*

FREE SCHOOL MILK

In the 1950s, all school children were given a free bottle of milk to drink during their mid-morning break. Crates of milk were delivered every morning, but there were no refrigerators to store them.

Teresa Martin's story

Teresa and her brother, Christopher, 1953

> *If the milk had been outside in the winter it would be frozen and it was put next to the boilers to defrost. The trouble was, it would do more than defrost, it would cook and be disgusting to drink.*

← Teresa (front, centre) and her classmates at St Richard's Primary School, Chichester.

OUTSIDE TOILETS

> The loos were freezing cold, very unfriendly places. You only went there if you desperately needed to go.

PEN AND INK

> The desks had a little inkwell. We had pen holders and a nib with two prongs. If you pressed too hard, the nib would scratch the paper and make a hole in it and you would get ink blots. I dreaded, dreaded handwriting, which you had to do every day.

ENGLISH

> We wrote lots of compositions with titles like 'A day in the life of a penny'. We also learned poetry and recited it together.

DISCIPLINE

> If you didn't work or you talked in class the teacher rapped your knuckles with a ruler. The worst thing was to be sent to the headteacher to be caned. I don't remember a girl being caned. The boys had to bend over to be caned on the behind. They would come back trying not to show that it hurt, but you could see that they had been crying.

← Each desk had its own ink well.

TIMES TABLES

> The teacher would walk up and down, swinging her arms in rhythm, chanting:
> 'One two is two,
> Two twos are four...'
> You had to keep in rhythm and you had to do it every day.

→ School reports were much briefer in the 1950s than they often are today.

WEST SUSSEX EDUCATION COMMITTEE

West Sussex County Council
St. Richard's R.C. School
55 St. Paul's Rd.,
Chichester.

..........SCHOOL

Summer TERM, 1955.

Name: *Teresa Allen*

Class: *Junior 3rd Form.* *Next Term Junior 2 Upper group.*

Number in Class:

		Assessment	Place in Class
Mental Arithmetic Mechanical & Problems	Excellent work	75	A
	Shows progress.	62	B
English	Reading: Excellent	100	A+
	Composition: More concentration needed	45	C
	Transcription: Writing very shaky	60	D
Geography, History and Social Studies	Quite good		B
	Very fair		B
Nature Study	Fair		
Art and Needlework Craft	Shows imagination	40	
	Teresa tries hard	75	A
		70	B
Physical Education and Games	Fair		B
Other Work	Religion: Excellent		A
	Poetry & Speech: Excellent	96	
	Dictation: } Excellent (but written	95	A
	Spelling: } badly)	77	A
General Remarks	Teresa needs to concentrate more. She has fretted over her mother this term and this has affected her work considerably.		

A = Very Good
B = Good
C = Average
D = Below Average
E = Very Weak

Signed: ....
Class Teacher.

Signed: *B. Easingwood-Wilson*
Headmaster/Headmistress.

(Please tear here)

11

Childhood

Terry remembers his childhood in the 1950s as, "Magical, ice-lolly filled times."

CRAZES

There were all kinds of crazes for collecting things in the 1950s, just as there are now.

Teresa remembers her brother playing with cigarette cards.

> *There were cards to collect which came in cigarette and tea packets. The boys would lay one card up against the wall and you'd have to flick another cigarette card at it. If you knocked it down then you could have it to add to your collection.*

HULA-HOOP

The hula-hoop craze from America caught on in Britain. You tried to whirl a brightly coloured hoop around your waist for as long as you could before it fell down.

⬇ Playing with hula hoops in Westerleigh School, Gloucestershire, 1953.

Fear of polio lifted

In the early 1950s, parents were fearful that their children would catch polio – a disease that could cause paralysis and even death. In 1953 a vaccination against polio was developed in America. Cynthia remembers her relief when she read the news.

"Polio was a big fear. I would never let my girls go to swimming baths or paddling pools or anywhere people said that polio could be picked up. When the polio vaccination came out, I remember feeling elated."

PLAYGROUND GAMES

Teresa remembers that the girls didn't play with the boys in the school playground.

We used to sit round in huddles playing five stones, cat's cradle or doing cotton reel sausage knitting or folding paper to make fortune tellers, well away from the boys playing football. We didn't run around very much. If we did get up and run around we used to do skipping. Sometimes we played juggling up in the air or against the wall with two balls. And handstands against the wall. You tucked your skirt into your revolting grey school knickers.

COMICS

Cynthia ordered *Girl* and *School Friend* every week for her daughters and bought them *The Beano*, *The Beezer* and *The Dandy* to make them laugh when they were ill.

→ *The Beano* and *The Dandy* were as popular in 1956 as they are today.

> **!** **Cynthia remembers...**
>
> *"Picnics were a great family thing, on the Downs or the beach. We went to the beach with a huge picnic box – sardine sandwiches, sausages, egg sandwiches, orange segments, chopped-up apples."*

Cynthia's children and their friends at the beach, 1953.

> **!** **Michael remembers ...**
>
> *"Train spotting meant seeing how many steam engines you could see. They may look the same but you knew they were different because they each had a different number. There was always an element of boasting about what you had seen that nobody else had. I still love steam trains even now."*

A new life in England

COMING TO BRITAIN

After the war and during the 1950s, many young men and women came to Britain from the Caribbean to find work and to make new lives for themselves and their families. Estel arrived in England from Jamaica in 1951.

> 66 *I came over because there wasn't any work in Jamaica. Things were tough at that time. I came on a plane from Jamaica. We were dispatched to different places but I went to Sunderland.* 99

Estel McDonald's story

Estel, 1958

⬇ Caribbean immigrants at Victoria station, London, 1956.

SNOW

In Sunderland, Estel went to work in a private school where she had her first experience of snow.

> 66 *The snow was so high, we used to wear long boots. We didn't have snow in Jamaica. You can imagine how hard it was. We had to shovel a path for the children.* 99

NO HOLIDAYS

Instead of taking time off during the school holidays, Estel took a second job.

> 66 *I went to a hotel in Scarborough to be a chambermaid. I worked because at that time I had my kids out in Jamaica. So you work and you send your money back for your kids.* 99

MOVING TO LONDON

After a year, Estel moved to London. Home was a single room.

> *It was only a small little room. We had a little gas ring. We'd put a penny in. We had a black lamp and a kettle to put on top of that lamp to get hot water to wash yourself with.*

TWO JOBS

Estel got two jobs. During the day she worked as a cleaner at Kingsmead, a retirement home in Chelsea. At four o'clock Estel caught the bus to her second job at a student's centre in Earl's Court where she worked all evening. Her day was very long.

> *I would catch the last tube home. I wasn't afraid because nobody would rob you. I had to get up at six o'clock again. I only had about five hours' sleep.*

BECOMING A NURSE

Soon Estel was able to give up her second job at the student centre.

> *The matron (at Kingsmead) called me one day and she said, 'Would you like to go on the nursing staff?' I said, 'Oh, very much'.*

Estel loved her job on the nursing staff.

> *I worked there for the rest of my working life.*

↓ Estel's family was eventually able to join her in England.

Estel (front left) with her children, 2001.

At work

HOUSEWIVES

Married women were less likely to go out to work in the 1950s than they are today. On average, a housewife worked fifteen hours a day shopping, cooking, washing and ironing and keeping the house clean. Cynthia remembers that it was a lot of work.

> 66 *I don't see how young mothers today with a job could possibly put in the time it took just to keep the house going – to keep things as they should be.* 99

↓ A teacher with a class at Mulbury Street Primary School, Hulme in 1956.

WOMEN AT WORK

In the 1950s men often expected their wives to stay at home, but increasingly women wanted to work outside the home. Michael remembers when his mother took a job as a secretary.

> 66 *I remember my father wasn't pleased. It was when men regarded themselves as the sole earner and it was thought to be 'infra dig' [unbecoming] if your wife worked.* 99

Brian's fiancée Joan trained to be a teacher. After they got married she did supply teaching in north London.

> 66 *I was teaching so I had a bit of money. I'd been to a Froebel college where the principle was learning through play. But when I started teaching, I had up to 50 in a class. Everything I learned at college went out of the window because with 50 six-year-olds, you had to do far more formal teaching.* 99

> **! Brian remembers...**
>
> His most important piece of office equipment was a very sharp pencil.
>
> *"After my Alternative National Service, I went straight into an architect's office. We sharpened our pencils with razor blades."*

AT THE OFFICE

One of the main differences between a 1950s office and a modern one is that there were no computers. A telephone and a typewriter would probably have been the most up-to-date technology. Secretaries had to have fast shorthand and typing speeds.

Coal and steel

In the 1950s whole communities depended on coal mining and the steel industry for work. The workers operated in dirty and dangerous conditions.

As a result of new fuels such as oil and gas, machinery replacing workers and competition from abroad, many mines and steel works that were thriving in the 1950s have now closed.

→ Steel workers worked with red-hot molten steel.

Terry Cowlishaw's story

Terry, 1958

ROCK 'N' ROLL

By the mid 1950s teenagers were dancing to a new kind of music called rock 'n' roll. Elvis Presley was rock 'n' roll king in America. Bill Haley and His Comets were the first American rock 'n' roll band to tour Britain, in 1957. They were met by large, enthusiastic crowds.

GOING TO CONCERTS

Terry went to see Ray Charles, Acker Bilk, Dave Brubeck and Dizzie Gillespie at De Montfort Hall in Leicester.

> *I booked for Cliff Richard and the Shadows in 1959, but the poor winter weather caused the show to be cancelled. You could get cheap tickets if you were prepared to stand in the side aisles or sit on the stage where I felt part of the proceedings and was able to see the drummers in fabulous close-up.*

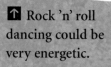

⬆ Rock 'n' roll dancing could be very energetic.

➡ Terry is still a big rock 'n' roll fan and plays the drums.

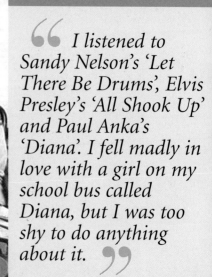

> *I listened to Sandy Nelson's 'Let There Be Drums', Elvis Presley's 'All Shook Up' and Paul Anka's 'Diana'. I fell madly in love with a girl on my school bus called Diana, but I was too shy to do anything about it.*

TEDDY BOYS

Terry's friend Colin was a Teddy Boy which involved a special kind of dress .

> *I wore a drape coat and drainpipe trousers, crêpe shoes, bootlace tie with my hair slicked back using Brylcreem and Vaseline. The hair was always specially important and was protected furiously from the wind and passing buses in case it was put out of place.*

Colin in his Teddy Boy gear.

Some hits of the 1950s

Lonnnie Donegan:
Rock Island Line

Bill Haley and His Comets:
Rock Around the Clock

Elvis Presley:
Heartbreak Hotel

Carl Perkins:
Blue Suede Shoes

Tommy Steele:
Singing the Blues

F. Lymon & the Teenagers:
Why Do Fools Fall in Love?

RIVAL GANGS

Colin was a member of a gang called the Leicester Townies. He remembers rocking and rolling in the aisles at the old Leicester Savoy cinema to the film 'Rock Around the Clock'. They went to dances at the Leicester Palais and hung out in coffee bars.

> *There were rival gangs in each town where we went and battles were frequent. There were even rival gangs in Leicester itself. Usually, gangs drank with each other after fighting. There was no continuing animosity afterwards – a fight one week and a drink together the next.*

Entertainment

LEISURE TIME

In the 1950s, more people than ever had time and money to spend on entertainment. Teenagers bought pop records, the cinema was popular and more and more homes had a television as well as a radio.

RADIO

Teresa liked to listen to the radio.

> " *There was the school quiz programme* Top of the Form – *one of my friends was in that. We liked the dramatisations of the children's stories about Jennings and Derbyshire at boarding school. There was Music While You Work, which used to be on in factories, but mums used to have it on while they were doing housework as well. So the radio was as significant a part of life as television is now.* "

↑ Children queue outside the Coliseum in Harrow Road, London to see Buster Crabbe in *Gun Brothers*.

CINEMA

Every Saturday morning, children all over the country queued up outside their local cinema for Saturday morning pictures. As well as episodes of cowboy films with Hopalong Cassidy or Roy Rogers, adventure films and comedy with Laurel and Hardy, there were yo-yo competitions and sing-a-longs.

↓ Radios were much larger in the 1950s than they are today.

! Michael remembers ...

"*They would have serials and each Saturday they would show an exciting episode and you would be left at the end of some crisis. My parents, who had a slightly puritan streak, wouldn't let me go to Saturday morning pictures every week, so the curse was, I only ever saw the serials with gaps in the middle. I never won the battle to go regularly.*"

TELEVISION

The BBC put out the first television broadcast in 1936. It wasn't until 1955 that Independent television (ITV) came on air showing the first television advertisements. Teresa's family didn't have a television until about 1957.

> 66 *I remember* Emergency Ward 10. *Everybody fell in love with the doctors.* 99

↑ In the 1950s many families bought their first television set.

GOING TO THE BALL

While Terry and Colin were rocking 'n' rolling in the aisles, Cynthia was dancing the quickstep, the waltz, the foxtrot and the tango at local balls. One year, the Queen came to the ball in Arundel, West Sussex.

> 66 *I remember someone saying, 'Stand back!' and she came sweeping through. She was in a fantastic dress of silver lace and taffeta. Her tiara, earrings and necklace were all diamonds and sapphires. She took your breath away.* 99

> 66 *Our dresses were the big thing. We thought about it for weeks beforehand. I had a fabulous dress of pink organza and lace. It had 40 yards of organza – long, to the ground. I had a different dress for every ball. Someone would make you a dress for about £2 and you could buy the material incredibly cheaply.* 99

← Cynthia at the ball wearing one of her favourite dresses.

The Festival of Britain

Michael, 1951

! Brian remembers...

Brian was an architectural student at the time. He was interested in the buildings.

"The Festival of Britain was a real eye opener. Brilliant designers showed us what life could offer. There were exciting buildings which were all fun and open. They used water and landscape and strong colours."

A TONIC FOR THE NATION

In 1851, over six million people visited the Great Exhibition in the Crystal Palace in London's Hyde Park. One hundred years later in 1951, the Festival of Britain helped people to forget the dark years of the war and to celebrate new ideas for an exciting future.

The main exhibition was on the South Bank of the River Thames in London but exhibitions and events were held all over the country. Michael lived in Wandsworth, London. He was one of the eight million visitors to the Festival.

> *I was first taken to the Festival of Britain by my parents and I liked it so much I went back a number of times.*
>
> *I remember the Skylon. It was a tall, elongated cigar-shaped thing that was suspended on a cradle and was a big landmark that could be seen for miles and miles.*

↓ The South Bank of the Thames during the Festival of Britain. The Skylon (to the right, with the Dome of Discovery behind) was 61 metres high. The Royal Festival Hall (square building, centre) is still used today for arts events and concerts.

22

← Many of the rides at Battersea Fun Fair had not been seen before in Britain.

BATTERSEA FUN FAIR

For Michael, the best part of the Festival of Britain was Battersea Fun Fair in Battersea Park. Fun fair attractions were brought over from America.

> *I loved it, particularly at night when it could be very crowded. Though I didn't have a lot of money it was fun to be in the mob and see all the stalls.*

THE DOME OF DISCOVERY

The Dome of Discovery documented British efforts to explore the Earth and Space.

> *There was a section in the Dome that was lit by ultraviolet light and I was wearing a white shirt. I just remember the shirt being absolutely brilliant white like you used to see in the old adverts for Daz.*
>
> *One of the interesting things is how modern it all seemed – it looks old-fashioned now.*

The Millennium Dome built for the Millennium celebrations in 2000 echoed the design of the 1951 Dome of Discovery.

> *I'd never seen the rides before. I remember the Wall of Death. You had a big cylinder with a floor and people stood against the wall. The thing started spinning and when it got to a critical speed the floor dropped out. The people were then pressed back against the wall and that was quite funny – they would get caught in the most amazing positions.*

THE EXHIBITION ENDS

After five months, the exhibition was torn down. Battersea Fun Fair lived on for many more years, but now only the Royal Festival Hall remains as a reminder of 1951's Festival of Britain on the South Bank.

Changing mood

A NEW ERA

The Festival of Britain helped to create a positive mood in Britain after the war. With the coronation of Queen Elizabeth II two years later, amazing new achievements and technological changes, people were enthusiastic about 'the new Elizabethan Age'.

⬇ Queen Elizabeth's Coronation was a spectacular event. It included a procession to and from the ceremony at London's Westminster Abbey.

THE CORONATION

The coronation of Queen Elizabeth II, on 2nd June 1953, was celebrated with bunting (flags threaded onto string) and street parties all over the country. Twenty million people watched it on television. Those who previously didn't own a TV set bought or hired one, and family and friends crowded round to see the fuzzy black and white pictures. Michael was there in person.

> ❝ *All the boys from our school lined up along the side of the road and we were given flags and told to wave. I remember the queen coming past and everybody had to wave and cheer.* ❞

Amazing achievements

Everest conquered

On 29th May 1953, a few days before the coronation, Edmund Hillary of New Zealand and Tenzing Norgay of Nepal became the first men in history to climb Mount Everest. News of this amazing achievement came through in time to add to the excitement of the coronation celebrations.

Four-minute mile

Athletes had been striving for so long to run a mile in under four minutes that it seemed an impossible achievement. But on 6th May 1954, British athlete Roger Bannister made history by running a mile in 3 minutes 59.4 seconds. By 1957, 16 more runners had followed in Bannister's footsteps and run the mile in under four minutes.

⬆ A Vespa, a popular scooter featured on a 1950s postcard.

⬇ Bubble cars had a door at the front, and the engine at the back.

GETTING AROUND

Motor scooters, bubble cars and Morris Minor cars all used very little petrol. They made it possible for many people to realise the dream of affording their own transport. Michael had a Lambretta scooter.

> ❝ *I used it in 1958 to go up and down to university. It was very cheap to run.* ❞

M1 OPENS

New roads had to be built to take the extra traffic. In 1959 Britain's first motorway, the M1, an 88-kilometre stretch of motorway going north from St Albans, was opened. At first about 13,000 vehicles travelled on it every day. Now the number is more than 88,000.

National Service

Brian, 1958

CALL UP

Between the end of the war and December 1960, all young men aged 18 were called up to do two years of National Service. The aim was for Britain's young men to be ready to go to war at a moment's notice. They joined the army, navy or air force and, after a few weeks' training, went into active service at home or abroad.

ALTERNATIVE NATIONAL SERVICE

Brian was studying architecture when he was called up, but National Service didn't fit in with his upbringing and beliefs. He was allowed to do 'Alternative National Service' instead. This meant he could do something worthwhile, but he didn't have to fight. He joined the Friends Ambulance Unit. After a year's service at home, Brian was sent to Austria. Brian then moved on to work in a refugee camp.

> *The Friends Ambulance Unit, the FAU, was set up for people who wanted to do something positive as an alternative to military service.*

> *We helped to erect prefabricated houses and were attached to the Swedish mission.*

← The Swedish Mission Headquarters in Austria where Brian lived.

> *Some of the refugees had been in forced labour camps and weren't in the best of health. These poor people would work building their houses in the day time and work in a local steel works at night to earn money to buy a bag of cement or two.*
>
> *One of these refugees who was building his house electrocuted himself, leaving his wife with an unfinished house. So we galloped to the rescue, finished the building and got her in just before the winter.*

↑ Refugee children playing near the camp where Brian and the FAU volunteers were living.

GO ANYWHERE, DO ANYTHING

> *One of the mottos of the FAU was GADA – go anywhere, do anything.*

One day, during the 1956 Hungarian uprising, Brian was asked to put GADA into practice.

> *I was helping preparing vegetables in the kitchen when suddenly Jack came in and said, 'They're desperate for medical supplies. If you go in half an hour's time to catch the train, you can pick up the medical supplies that they want.' We just got in and got the supplies to them.*

→ The Müllers' house was only half built, before the volunteers stepped in.

← Fr Müller (left) was very grateful for the help she was given. She is shown here with two of the men from the unit. The other woman and child are her family.

Brian's experiences in the FAU were some of the most memorable of his life. He still keeps up with news of the unit and his old friends.

⬆ H-bomb tests in the Pacific produced massive mushroom clouds, pictures of which were seen all round the world.

THE COLD WAR

Rivalry between the two super-powers, the Soviet Union and the United States, and the powerful new hydrogen and atom bombs brought the fear of global disaster. The two powers didn't directly use weapons against each other but, between the end of World War II and 1989, they fought what was know as the 'Cold War'. It was conducted through spying, arms build-up and propaganda.

H-BOMB TESTED

In 1952, the Americans tested the H-bomb (H for hydrogen) on an uninhabited Pacific island. A radioactive mushroom cloud rose 40 kilometres into the air and the whole island disappeared under the sea.

! Cynthia remembers...
"All the joy of the family and the things we did together was coloured tremendously by the Cold War and by fear of the A-bomb and the H-bomb and what the Russians would do."

THE ALDERMASTON MARCH

The first big anti-nuclear march from London to Aldermaston, where nuclear weapons are researched, took place in 1958. The marchers were calling for a ban on nuclear weapons.

> **! Brian remembers…**
> "I didn't join CND (Campaign for Nuclear Disarmament) marches because I preferred to be doing something constructive with a few people. After I'd finished my alternative to military service I was just anxious to get back into architecture."

⬆ Demonstrators on the Aldermaston march – the first time the now familiar 'ban the bomb' symbol was seen.

THE SPACE RACE

The United States and the Soviet Union were involved in another kind of rivalry – the race to be the first to explore space and to land on the Moon. It was known as the 'space race'.

SPUTNIK

The Soviet Union made the first breakthrough when, in 1957, it launched 'Sputnik 1', the first artificial satellite. Cynthia's daughter remembers her father showing her how to spot Sputnik moving slowly across the night sky.

> ❝ Dad set a telescope up in the garden and trained it on what looked like a very bright star. It was amazing to think we were looking at the very first object human beings had ever put into space. ❞

Space race facts
• •

1957 The Soviet Union launch the first artificial satellite into space.

1958 The United States launch its first artificial satellite into space – Explorer 1.

1959 The Americans train seven men to go into space.

1959 A Russian satellite takes the first pictures of the other side of the moon.

The space race went on into the 1960s when the Soviet Union was the first to send a man into space, but the United States achieved the first manned moon landing.

Timeline

1950
24th February Labour wins general election under Clement Attlee.

1951
January US atom bomb tests in Nevada desert.
4th May Opening of Festival of Britain.
26th October Conservatives win election, Winston Churchill is prime minister again.

1952
6th February King George VI dies.
30th November Hydrogen bomb tests on Eniwetok Atoll in the Pacific Ocean.

1953
29th May Everest conquered for the first time by Edmund Hillary and Tenzing Norgay.
2nd June Coronation of Elizabeth II.
August Russia becomes a nuclear power.

1954
12th April Bill Haley and His Comets record 'Rock Around the Clock'.
26th April Trials of polio vaccine.
6th May British athlete Roger Bannister runs a mile in 3 minutes 59.4 seconds.
3rd July Food rationing comes to an end.

1955
5th April Winston Churchill resigns as prime minister and is succeeded by Sir Anthony Eden.
22nd September Independent television – ITV – broadcasts for the first time.

1956
5th July Clean Air Act passed. Burning coal fires in cities banned.
26th July The Egyptian president nationalises the Suez canal, sparking the three-month long 'Suez Crisis'.
26th October Hungarians rise up against Russian invasion.
5th November Hungarians are defeated.

1957
10th January Sir Anthony Eden resigns and Harold Macmillan becomes prime minister.
25th March The Treaty of Rome is signed and the European Common Market is set up.
4th October Russia launches Sputnik 1, the first artificial satellite, into space.

1958
7th April Aldermaston March against nuclear weapons.
22nd October Bubble car displayed at the Motor Show.

1959
18th August New mini cars launched.
14th September Russian space craft Lunik 2 is the first artificial object to land on the Moon.
22nd November Opening of M1 motorway.

Glossary

Bronchitis Inflammation of the tubes that carry air to the lungs.

Brylcreem A kind of hair cream for men. It holds hair in place and makes it shine.

Cat's cradle A game where two people hold a circle of string between them and pass it to each other, changing the pattern each time.

Chambermaid Someone who cleans hotel bedrooms.

Combined Cadet Force (CCF) An organisation for young trainees for the army, navy and air force.

Commonwealth A group of countries that all have a shared part in British history.

Coupons Ration books contained printed bits of paper called coupons. Coupons were exchanged for food, clothes or fuel.

Hungarian Uprising In 1956, Hungarian people demonstrated against Russian troops in their country. They were defeated by Russian bombs and tanks.

National Service The call up by the government of young men to go into the army, navy or air force for a length of time.

Nuclear disarmament A call for countries to give up all their nuclear weapons.

Nuclear weapons Weapons that have very high explosive power.

Organza A very fine transparent silk.

Partition A moveable wall that can make one large room into two smaller rooms.

Prefabricated The walls and roof of a prefabricated house are made in a factory. They can be put together quickly on site.

Propaganda Radio and television broadcasts, films and leaflets that put over a government's message to the people.

Puritan Someone with very strict standards of behaviour.

Radioactive Nuclear bombs give out invisible radioactivity which can cause damaging changes in the human body.

Rations Set amounts of food, clothes or fuel that people are allowed during times when there is a shortage of these things.

Satellite An object that orbits the Earth.

Shorthand A fast way of writing using symbols for whole words and phrases.

Superpowers Very powerful countries with nuclear weapons.

Twin-tub A machine with two tubs: one for washing and rinsing, the other for spin drying.

Vaccination Something given to protect against a disease.

Index